Born Too

A practical guide for parents of
babies born prematurely

———

000

PETE MOORE

Thorsons
An Imprint of HarperCollins*Publishers*

The information provided in this book is for guidance purposes only. Please ensure that you follow the advice given you by the medical experts in charge of your baby's care.

Thorsons
An Imprint of HarperCollins*Publishers*
77–85 Fulham Palace Road,
Hammersmith, London W6 8JB
1160 Battery Street,
San Francisco, California 94111–1213

Published by Thorsons 1995

10 9 8 7 6 5 4 3 2 1

© Pete Moore 1995

Pete Moore asserts the moral right to
be identified as the author of this work

A catalogue record for this book
is available from the British Library

ISBN 0 7225 3229 6

Text illustrations by Angela Christie

Printed in Great Britain by
HarperCollinsManufacturing Glasgow

Contents

List of Illustrations

Acknowledgements

Action Research would like to thank the following experts for their help in putting this book together. Without their enthusiasm, this book would not have been possible.

Dee Beresford	Project Co-ordinator Nottingham Neonatal Services
Doreen Crawford	Senior Clinical Nurse Leicester Royal Infirmary
Professor Henry Halliday	Consultant Neonatologist Royal Maternity Hospital, Belfast
Paula Hale	Senior Nurse Manager City Hospital, Nottingham
Dr Pete Hope	Consultant Paediatrician The John Radcliffe, Oxford
Alixe Kent	Principal Clinical Psychologist Hammersmith Hospitals NHS Trust
Dr Neil Marlow	Consultant Senior Lecturer St Michael's Hospital, Bristol
Heather Naylor	Neonatal Community Specialist Hammersmith Hospitals NHS Trust
Dr Janet Rennie	Consultant in Neonatal Medicine Addenbrooke's Hospital, Cambridge

Professor Charles Rodeck	Professor of Obstetrics and Gynaecology University College London
Mr John Spencer	Consultant Obstetrician and Gynaecologist Northwich Park and St Mark's NHS Trust, Harrow
Sylvia Watson	Senior Neonatal Nurse Hammersmith Hospitals Trust
Dr John Wyatt	Consultant Neonatal Paediatrician University College London

The Special Care Baby Unit at
Crawley General Hospital
The Royal College of Midwives

We would also particularly like to thank Professor of Child Health at the University of Leicester, Mike Silverman, for overseeing the project, and the other experts and the many parents of premature babies whose suggestions and comments guided our thoughts.

`Preface`

Congratulations on the birth of your child!

My daughter Katie was born seven weeks too early. It was a great shock as I, like you, did not think it would happen to me.

Having gone through the experience, my heart goes out to other parents going through this time of joy mixed with terrible anguish.

One of the things I hated most was feeling helpless and not in control. There was very little information available to help. I am just so grateful to the hospital staff for all their love and care.

I think that this book produced by Action Research is wonderful and know it will be of enormous help to you. It will give you a better understanding of what you and your child are going through and what you are likely to experience in the coming weeks. It will help you to communicate better with the doctors and nurses caring for your child as you will be more aware and, as a result, more in control. I wish *Born Too Early* had been around for me.

Very best wishes,

Carol Vorderman

Introduction

For most of us, the first nine months of our lives are spent protected in our mother's womb. Over this time we grow from a microscopic single cell to a fully active baby, capable of breathing, eating and regulating most body mechanisms. Birth then is a relatively simple transition into a world for which we have been fully prepared.

But for about 5 per cent of babies, the period of protected isolation is abruptly cut short as they enter the world a few months early. Weighing as little as 500 grams (1 lb), these babies have to fight for their lives. Their lungs are not ready, their brains are not fully formed and even their skin is fragile.

For the family of a newly born premature baby, this is a time of extreme trauma. Parents are amazed to see their tiny baby, but fearful of the future. Family and friends may feel awkward; after all, should they congratulate the parents, or commiserate?

Action Research spends millions of pounds funding research which continually improves the way that doctors and nurses can care for these babies. Drawing on the expertise and experience of research workers funded by the charity and other friends, we have compiled this comprehensive guide to the care of premature babies, to help parents, family and friends.

We hope this book will encourage you, as you see how much help is available. The book should be used as a reference source to back up and explain what doctors and nurses tell you. It lists a wide range of medical complications, but you must not be drawn into thinking that your baby will suffer from them all. Every baby is different and will have a unique set of strengths and weaknesses.

Throughout the book we refer to the baby as 'he'. We have not forgotten that about half of all premature babies are girls, and the information provided is just as applicable to them. However, using this format makes certain parts easier to read, as 'he' always refers to the baby, 'she' to the mother.

I hope you will find this book useful and reassuring. Having visited many neonatal units around the country, I am confident that the care and attention you and your baby will receive will be the best.

Our thoughts and best wishes are with you.

Anne Luther
Director General — Action Research

Your Baby

Names ....

....

....

Born on
    Day ....
    Date ....
    Time ....

Measurements
    Weight ....
    Length ....

Useful names of staff
    Consultant Obstetrician ....
    Senior Registrar ....
    Midwife ....
    Nursing team ....

    On the baby unit
    Consultant Paediatrician ....
    Senior Registrar ....
    Nursing team ....
        Primary nurse ....

....

Useful telephone numbers
Baby unit ....

....

....

....

....

———

Chapter Two

Premature Birth –
Some Facts and Figures

Right at the start it would be good to sort out an area of confusion — the difference between the terms 'low birth weight babies' and 'premature babies'. Any baby born before 37 weeks of pregnancy have been completed is called *premature* or *preterm*. Any baby born weighing less than 2,500 g (5½ lb) is said to have a *low birth weight*. You may come across the term *very low birth weight*, which is reserved for babies born weighing less than 1,500 g (3 lb).

Almost all premature babies are also low birth weight. However, the two terms cannot be used interchangeably, as some full-term babies are very small when they are born, and so they are also called low birth weight babies.

Every year over 700,000 babies are born in the UK, and of these 70,000 (one in ten) are admitted to a special care baby unit. Over half of these babies are admitted because they have been born prematurely.

The closer a baby is to full term when he is born, the greater his chances of surviving. While less than a half of babies born between 23 and 25 weeks survive, most babies born over 28 weeks and admitted to a neonatal unit survive. Of these, 90 per cent grow up with no noticeable disability.

Basic Causes of Premature Birth

There is no one reason for preterm births, just as there is no uniform outcome for a premature baby. Many different things may trigger a preterm birth, some of which we know about and some we do not. However, most premature births can be divided into one of four groups.

1. Unexplained Preterm Labour with Intact Membranes

A Complete Surprise

Between a quarter and a third of all premature births occur for no apparent reason, and often with no warning. Some doctors now think that many of these births may be stimulated by an undetected infection.

A vaginal swab may be taken when the mother first arrives in hospital to see if there is any sign of an infection. If an infection is detected, doctors may try to delay labour and treat any infection using antibiotics.

These premature deliveries often cause most problems, as the mother is not fully prepared for the baby to arrive. While hospitals are always prepared to cope with premature births, it can take a few minutes to get all of the relevant staff collected together.

2. Rupture of Membranes (Breaking Waters) with or without Labour

Starting Too Soon

In the mother's womb, the baby lies in a pool of fluid contained in a membrane sac. Normally the membrane only breaks once labour has started. But in about 10 per cent of all pregnancies the membranes rupture before labour starts. If this happens before 37 weeks, then the mother is more likely to have a premature delivery.

In particular circumstances doctors may give the mother a drug to delay labour for a couple of days and another drug to help mature the baby's lungs before birth.

A Weak Cervix

Sometimes the membranes rupture and the baby is born early because the neck of the womb, the cervix, is weak and opens up (dilates) too early. If your doctor thinks that this was the problem, he or she may recommend that a stitch is inserted next time you are pregnant to prevent a premature delivery or miscarriage.

3. Elective Delivery

A Vital Decision

As neonatal intensive care improves, doctors are more confident about delivering babies early. They will do this if mother or baby appears to be in danger should the pregnancy continue.

Doctors have to juggle between two different aspects:

1. The womb is normally the best place for your baby to develop. Doctors will do all that they can to slow down an early labour and allow the longest possible time for your

baby to develop in the womb.
2. However, sometimes mother or baby may be in danger if the pregnancy is allowed to continue. There may then be no option but to deliver the baby early and continue caring for him in a neonatal unit.

There are two main reasons why doctors may decide to deliver a baby early:

1. The mother may have been suffering from pre-eclampsia.
2. Your baby may have stopped growing, suggesting that there is something wrong with the placenta.

Making a positive decision to deliver your baby has several advantages. One of the most important is that a team of appropriate specialists can be assembled so that both mother and baby receive the best attention possible.

Once the baby is born, doctors may be in a better position to treat any problems that he may have.

4. Emergency Delivery

A Time to Act

A quarter of all premature babies are born because of an obstetric emergency such as bleeding (antepartum haemorrhage) or a problem with the umbilical cord. Normally such deliveries are made by a caesarean section.

Delaying Labour

Buying Time

Doctors are highly skilled at looking after babies born before they are due. However, they cannot match the nurture provided by a healthy womb. Even with specialized nutrition, babies do not always thrive as well once delivered as they would have if they had remained inside. So, wherever possible, doctors will try to postpone labour for as long as possible. A group of drugs called *beta mimetics* can help delay labour. Doctors may also give the mother antibiotics just in case the onset of labour was caused by a mild infection.

Even a couple of days can make a lot of difference. It may provide enough time to transfer the mother to a specialist centre, and the extra time can be used to stimulate baby's lungs to mature more quickly. This is achieved by giving the mother a drug called *betamethasone* or *dexamethasone*. This drug passes across the placenta and stimulates cells in your baby's lungs, so that they will be ready to cope with breathing air. This drug is quite safe and simply stimulates a natural process which would have occurred a few weeks later if your baby had not been born prematurely.

By helping lungs to mature more quickly, steroids like betamethasone:

- reduce the problems that premature babies have with breathing by 50 per cent
- reduce the risk of your baby suffering from bleeding in the brain (intraventricular haemorrhage) over the first few days and weeks after birth.

Pre-eclampsia

also called 'pregnancy induced hypertension'

Pre-eclampsia occurs in about 1 in 14 pregnancies. It can be a dangerous condition if it is not recognized and treated.

If the condition is not controlled it can lead to strokes, eclamptic fits, heart failure, kidney failure and blood clotting problems in the mother. This is dangerous for both mother and baby.

Pre-eclampsia only goes away once the placenta is removed. For this to happen the baby must be delivered.

Some mothers are upset because their baby has suddenly been born by a caesarean section. However, if pregnancy had been allowed to continue, then the health of both they and their babies would have been badly affected.

Pre-eclampsia can come on in hours, but normally takes a few days or even weeks to appear. The reason why pre-eclampsia happens is poorly understood. Many people, some funded by Action Research, are actively involved in research to try to remove the problem.

Pre-eclampsia is:

- more common in a woman's first pregnancy
- more common in young women
- more common in mothers carrying more than one baby.

Pre-eclampsia is almost always a problem associated with first pregnancies and rarely occurs in subsequent ones, even if a woman suffered from it in her first.

Warning Signs

A rise in blood pressure measured at an antenatal clinic could be the first sign of problems. Protein starts to appear in urine — again, this can be detected at the clinic. The mother may also notice that her arms and legs are swelling up (peripheral oedema).

Other symptoms that may come on rapidly:

- blurred vision
- headaches
- abdominal pain
- nausea.

Severe abdominal pain may also be a sign of labour.

Mothers-to-be who have one or more of these symptoms are advised to go and see their doctor or midwife quickly.

Chapter Four

000

The First Day

Not all parents have a warning that their baby is going to arrive early. But whether you have known for a few weeks, a few days, or just a few hours, the first day is full of anxiety and shock. You are likely to experience emotions you did not realize were possible.

You may be shocked when you first see your baby. Few very premature babies look particularly beautiful. They are delicate and incredible, but look quite different from any baby that you have seen before. They are very different to the smiling, chubby babies that you will see in most magazines and adverts. You may not even be able to see your baby's face, hidden away behind a mass of tubes and sticking plaster and wearing a bonnet to keep his head warm. Often premature babies have a fine covering of dark hair all over their bodies, including their faces.

Do not worry. Your baby looks just like any other baby does at this stage of development. The only difference is that he is outside so you can see him clearly. Over the next few months he will grow and start to look more like all other babies.

Before your baby is born, you may be visited by a paediatrician. This is a doctor whose special skill is looking after babies. He or she will spend time discussing the different things that may happen once your baby is born, and get an idea of how you would like them to be handled.

A paediatrician will be at the delivery of your baby.

As soon as your baby is born, doctors will assess his health. They will be looking at:

- heart beat
- breathing
- overall colour — which indicates how much oxygen is in the baby's bloodstream
- his general level of activity.

If your baby is not breathing well, a member of staff may put a tube down through his nose or mouth into his lungs and start to help his breathing straight away.

It is very important that your baby is kept warm at this stage. As he will be wet, there will be a real problem of heat loss until he has been thoroughly dried.

If doctors need to carry out any emergency treatments, these will be started immediately. You will be kept informed of your baby's condition.

Moving On

Into Intensive Care

It will usually be possible for the parents to see their baby before he is taken to intensive care. However, this will not always be the case if the baby is particularly unwell, or if the mother has had a general anaesthetic.

Whatever happens, fathers have a much greater chance of seeing the baby over the first few hours. There will always be a Polaroid camera available for photographs to be taken so that the mother can see her baby even if she cannot come to the neonatal unit.

Your baby will be transferred to the neonatal unit when his condition is stable.

Mothers may occasionally be brought around to neonatal units to see their babies before going to the ward to rest. However, in most cases they need to rest for at least a few hours first. Then they will be taken there in a wheelchair or, if necessary, in their bed. They probably will not have enough energy to spend very long with their babies at this point, but fathers may want to stay longer.

At this stage there will be very little that fathers can do for their babies. But they are very welcome to stay for as long as they like. If a father feels that he either wants to go away, or needs to go away because of other family commitments, he should not feel guilty. As a father you may feel torn between two patients, your wife and your newborn. The hospital staff are there to look after your baby.

Moving Hospitals

The Flying Squad

Local hospitals that do not have intensive care facilities will make every effort to transfer mothers to hospitals that have specialist intensive care facilities before the babies are born. This is because babies are much safer while they are still inside their mothers' wombs, rather than in incubators.

However, if this has not been possible it may be necessary to move your baby to another hospital after the birth. This usually happens on the first day. It may then be a couple of days before the mother is well enough to move to the same hospital.

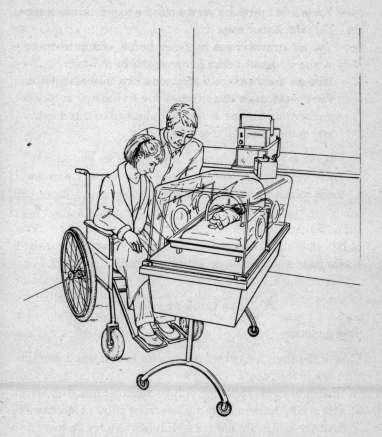

Many mothers make their first visit in a wheelchair.

What Next?

Welcome to the Unit

- You will be introduced to the nurse who will be taking special care of your baby.
- You will be given some brief instructions, such as where to wash your hands before touching your baby.
- Mothers are then usually allocated a bed on another ward.
- Fathers can stay in the intensive care unit as long as they like — they may even be allocated a guest bed so that they can stay in the hospital if they wish.

A nurse will take photographs of your baby for you to keep. These can be particularly comforting for mothers who are too ill to visit the intensive care unit.

TIP: *It is a good idea to carry a camera with you when you visit your baby — you can't have too many photos!*

A Close Look at your Baby

Taking Stock

One of the first things that doctors do is to insert a fine tube into one of the baby's veins. This may be in a hand, foot, scalp or umbilical cord. This tube will be attached to a drip which slowly sends nutrients directly into your baby's bloodstream. Premature babies are not born with large stores of energy, so a continuous supply of glucose (the form of sugar that travels around the bloodstream as a ready supply of energy) is very important.

- Doctors may also place another tube into an artery, sometimes via the umbilical cord.
- Electrodes with sticky pads will be placed on your baby's chest to monitor his heart.
- Your baby's temperature will also be monitored carefully.
- Saturation monitors constantly detect the amount of oxygen in your baby's blood.
- Your baby's blood pressure will be measured regularly.

Blood Tests

Blood samples will be taken every few hours, more often if there is any uncertainty. Samples are collected either by drawing blood out of one of the tubes or by making a small prick in the baby's heel.

Is our Baby Uncomfortable?

Placing tubes in your baby may cause him slight distress. However, once the tubes have been placed into your baby he will not find them too uncomfortable. If he shows signs of distress and tries to move a lot then he may be gently sedated with medication. This is important so that he does not pull the tubes out and possibly damage himself.

One of the aims of the medical staff when babies are very small is to try and keep handling them to a minimum in order to reduce their discomfort.

Why Can't I Hold my Baby?

At this stage, handling and cuddling your baby may worsen his condition. If your baby is well enough, you may be able to cradle his head in your hand. Once your baby is stable, you may be able to hold and cuddle him even if he is attached to a ventilator.

This does not mean that you cannot touch him. If you would like, having washed your hands, you may gently touch or stroke him.

What Can We Do?

There is very little at this stage that parents can do. However, mothers can help by expressing breastmilk, if they had planned to breastfeed the baby. Using an electric breast pump is the easiest, if not always the most comfortable way; depending on your hospital you may need to hire one. Your midwife will give you all the help you need and tell you how to get hold of one. Any milk you express will be frozen so that it is ready for your baby to have at a later date.

As soon as your baby is stable enough for you to join in providing care, the nurses will be only too pleased to show you what you can do to help. This won't take long, but you will need to be patient at first. For the first few days, even the medical staff will be trying to disturb your baby as little as possible.

How Much Can my Baby Tell about the World Around Him?

If he is not on a ventilator with a tube in his windpipe, he will be able to cry. Because he is so small his cry will sound quite strange.

He will slowly start to learn to recognize voices. This does not happen immediately, but this is no surprise as even a full-term baby probably takes a few days or weeks to learn to recognize voices.

Unless he is on medication that keeps him calm, he may open his eyes occasionally and be able to see a little.

How Much Do We Know about our Baby's Health?

Doctors will only be able to tell you how your baby is from day to day. It is very difficult at this stage to say anything about the likely long-term outcome. One day your baby may be doing well, the next he may be ill. Then again a few days later he may be doing well again.

Asking Questions

Do not worry if you ask some questions over and over again because you have not understood or cannot remember the answer. There is so much around that is new that it will be impossible for you to take it in all at once. All staff will understand this and will be only too happy to answer again questions that they may have already answered before.

It is worth writing down any questions that you think of in advance so that you do not forget them once you have an opportunity to ask someone. In the same way, it is also worth writing down the answers to some of your more complex questions. This way you can read them over later on.

Finding your Way Around

Feeling at Home

Most hospitals have accommodation so that both parents can stay at the hospital for the first couple of days.

Look around the unit and find out where you can get refreshments. The unit may have a small sitting-room or coffee room for parents to use. There is usually a book case containing useful leaflets and information.

Whom Can We See?

Help from the Community

Ask to see anyone that you would like, such as any religious or community leader. A Community Liaison Midwife is also available, offering counselling and support to parents both in the unit and once they are at home. The unit will have a list of relevant contact names and phone numbers. You will be surprised how willing people are to help.

What Tests Are Needed?

There is no fixed set of tests that doctors and nurses always perform on babies born prematurely. As a rule, the less your baby is disturbed the happier and healthier he will be. Doctors carry out the minimum number of tests they need to help them look after your baby.

Each baby will have a unique set of problems and will need a unique combination of tests. The healthier and bigger your baby is, the less monitoring he will require.

Preterm babies are often very ill, and therefore full intensive care offers the best chance of success and involves continuous monitoring.

So, Are Tests Routine?

The fact that doctors are performing tests does not mean that there is a problem. More often than not, tests are carried out to ensure that your baby is progressing well and to see if any minor adjustments to medical care would be helpful. Some tests are carried out every three or four hours, while others occur only every few days or weeks.

Equipment and Its Functions

Monitoring and Supporting your Baby

IV Lines

Very small premature babies are born before their stomachs and gut are fully developed. As a result it may be impossible to deliver all the nutrients the baby needs by mouth.

Instead, doctors insert fine tubes directly into your baby's veins. They may place them in your baby's arm or through the umbilical cord. These tubes are sometimes called 'catheters' or 'lines'. They can then pass nutrients such as glucose and amino acids (the building blocks for proteins) into your baby's bloodstream, bypassing the gut. This is a very efficient way of giving your baby the food that he needs in order to grow.

In order to help gut development, nurses may feed your baby a small amount of milk – no greater than a teaspoonful (1 — 5 ml). This will stimulate hormones which help his bowels to mature. The best milk to use for this is breastmilk, as it has a perfect balance of protein and sugars. Furthermore, even such a small amount of breastmilk will help to protect your baby against infections. If you cannot express milk, the hospital may be able to supply some breastmilk from a milk-bank.

Blood Pressure

Measuring blood pressure is a good index of general health. A tube in one of your baby's arteries makes it possible to monitor his blood pressure continuously. If an arterial catheter is not in use, then nurses will regularly measure your baby's blood pressure using a miniature pressure-cuff.

Heart Monitors

If doctors have put a tube into one of your baby's arteries, they can monitor his heart rate using the same machine that monitors blood pressure. The machine counts pressure-pulses that occur each time the heart beats.

Another system measures the electrical activity of the heart. This ECG monitor works by detecting currents that occur with each heart beat. To record this, nurses will stick two or three electrodes on your baby's chest.

Blood Tests

It is quite normal for doctors and nurses to take frequent blood samples. Often this is carried out by making a small prick in your baby's heel. If a small tube has been placed into one of your baby's arteries or veins, they may be able to take samples from there, instead of making a heel prick.

They will be measuring:

- glucose
- blood salts
- blood gases — to adjust any oxygen supply or the ventilator, if your baby is on one
- haemoglobin — to see whether your baby is anaemic
- platelets — small fragments of cells that are needed to prevent bleeding. They are often in short supply in premature babies.

Monitoring Oxygen Levels

To help premature babies whose lungs have not fully developed, doctors may supply them with extra oxygen. However, it is important that the babies do not get too much, as this may be damaging, especially to their eyes. The amount of oxygen in your baby's blood will therefore be monitored very carefully using one of three different techniques: a pulse oximeter, transcutaneous monitoring, or continuous indwelling arterial probe.

Pulse Oximeters

— Pulse oximeters shine light through the skin and monitor the blood's colour. When blood has a lot of oxygen in it, it turns red; when there is less oxygen it is bluish in colour.

Transcutaneous Monitoring

— This machine warms a small area of skin and increases blood flow at the surface. It then measures how much oxygen is in that blood. The probe leaves a harmless red mark that soon disappears.

Continuous Indwelling Arterial Probe

— This is a special tube with a miniature sensor built into the end. The tube is inserted into an artery, where it measures how much oxygen is in the baby's blood.

Ultrasound Scans

Normally, doctors will scan your baby's brain once a week. If medical staff suspect that there is a problem they may perform a scan once a day. They use a machine that is very similar to the one that may have been used to see your baby before he was born.

Brain ultrasounds are often carried out to see if there are any areas of bleeding or bruising within the brain. This bleeding may occur because areas of the brain have not finished developing fully and are extremely fragile.

Bleeding in the brain occurs in about 25 per cent of very

premature babies. However, in most cases the bleeding is only slight and does not cause any long-term problems.

If the scan is clear, does that mean that my baby is definitely OK?

Bleeding is not the only cause of problems in premature babies, and unfortunately a normal scan is not an absolute guarantee of full health. This is discussed in more detail on *page 81*.

X-rays

X-ray photographs are often taken to check the positions of the tips of the catheters and breathing tube that doctors have put in your baby. It is very important that the ends of these tubes are in the right place. X-ray photographs are also used to keep an eye on any lung damage, and to help in the search for any other of the wide range of problems that may develop in the baby's chest and tummy.

The machine used is portable and is brought to your baby. It uses the lowest dose of X-rays possible. The risk to your baby from the radiation is very small.

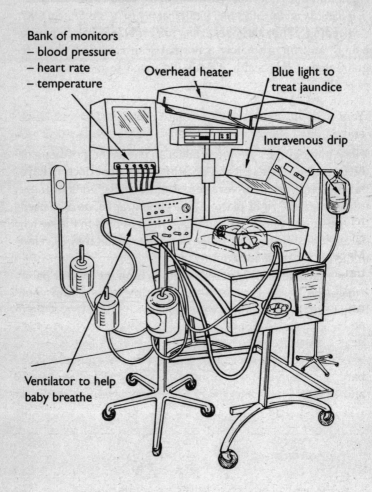

Bank of monitors
– blood pressure
– heart rate
– temperature

Overhead heater

Blue light to
treat jaundice

Intravenous drip

Ventilator to help
baby breathe

*So much equipment. It can be quite difficult to see your baby
in the midst of all this technology.*

Life in Special Care Baby Units

Your baby may be in a part of the hospital called one of several things: a neonatal unit, a neonatal intensive care unit, or a special care baby unit. All these different names describe an area of the hospital dedicated to treating your baby with the special care that he needs because he was born early.

A premature baby needs looking after in ways that are different to those needed by a sick child or adult. Doctors in charge of your baby's care are specialists in the care of babies. Many of the nurses, especially the senior ones, will have been trained specifically in looking after sick and premature babies.

Because your baby was born prematurely, his organs may not be fully mature. Special care baby units have equipment and skilled staff to support your baby until all his organs have developed more fully.

While the nurses on the baby unit are looking after your baby, your midwife will continue to visit you for between 10 and 28 days after the delivery. After this, your Health Visitor will get in touch.

Help with Breathing

- The lungs of premature babies are not usually fully developed.
- Special equipment in the unit will help your baby breathe.
- This will give your baby's lungs time to continue developing.

Help with Keeping Warm

- Very immature babies need help keeping warm.
- The smaller and weaker a baby is, the more heating is needed.
- As your baby matures, less heat will be required.
- Your baby will not be washed for a number of days or even weeks, because when the water evaporates the baby becomes cool and this must be avoided.

Help with Feeding

- Many premature babies cannot suck adequately.
- They may need feeding through a tube passed through their mouth or nose into their stomach.

If a baby is extremely small or unwell, doctors may place a tube into a vein and feed nutrients directly into his blood using an intravenous drip.

When Can We See our Baby?

Visiting Times

Most baby units encourage parents to visit their baby as soon as possible after the birth. If your baby was born by caesarean section, it is sometimes a number of hours, occasionally days, before the mother is able to visit. However, it is good for you, and for your baby, if you see him as soon as you are able.

You will be encouraged to visit your baby as often as possible and stay as long as you wish. At first, short but frequent visits may be easiest. However, once the mother has been discharged from hospital, this may not be possible. You may have to make fewer, more prolonged visits.

Parents are encouraged to bring any of the baby's brothers

and sisters to see him, but other children who are not family members are generally not allowed in baby units. This is in order to reduce the chance of introducing childhood infections into the unit. Most units allow adult friends and relatives to visit, but only if they are accompanied by one of the baby's parents. There may also be a limit to the number of people who can see the baby at any one time.

If you cannot visit, keep in touch by phone. Baby units are active day and night, so feel free to telephone at any time to ask how your baby is. Some parents find comfort in phoning just before they go to bed and as soon as they wake up.

Some parents find that visiting the unit can be difficult because they are frightened that they may be greeted with bad news. Telephoning before setting out to the hospital, and therefore knowing in advance what your baby's condition is, can help ease this kind of anxiety.

Hospital Security

It is most important that you observe all instructions related to security. Remember that any regulations and precautions are there to protect you and your baby. Do everything you can to help by keeping to any rules. Please let the staff on the unit know each time you arrive and also when you go home.

How Long Will our Baby Be in the Special Care Unit?

The Long Haul

This is impossible to predict, but if all goes well your baby is likely to be ready to go home near to the date he was originally due to be born.

- Occasionally he might go home up to a month earlier than his original due date.

- If your baby has been particularly sick, he may not be ready to go home for some weeks after he was due to be born.

When Is an Alarm not Alarming?

The Bells, the Bells!

Special care baby units are full of technical equipment. These machines are there to help nurses and doctors look after the babies, and almost every piece of equipment has alarms for safety reasons so that staff can respond quickly.

Alarms watch over both baby and machines. Because they are very sensitive, they may go off at the slightest change. This means that they will sometimes sound when there is nothing wrong. Just as sensitive car alarms can go off even when there has been no attempt to tamper with it, the alarms on the technical equipment in a special care unit can be triggered accidentally.

While some alarms demand an immediate response, the doctors and nurses are able to recognize inappropriate alarms. Nurses and doctors will always tell you what machines do and how they work, but it is their job, not yours, to respond to alarms.

Remember that these machines are only there to help the doctors and nurses. It is their expert supervision, and your loving care, that are of greatest importance to your baby.

How Do I Avoid Passing an Infection to my Baby?

Keeping Clean

- Always wash your hands on your arrival at the unit.
- Exclude other visitors who have coughs, colds or cold sores.

- However, if you have a minor cold, it is probably more beneficial for your baby to see you than for you to stay away. Simply stay away from any other babies in the unit.
- Babies pick up childhood infections very easily, so it is safer not to bring any children, other than brothers and sisters, to the unit.
- A few units ask visitors to wear gowns/other protective clothing.

What Staff Are There in Special Care Baby Units?

Nurses

Many of the nurses in special care units have been specially trained to look after premature and sick babies.

Any trainee nurses will already have qualified as general nurses and will be undergoing closely supervised additional training in caring for sick and premature babies. Some trainee nurses may be on the unit purely to observe.

At any one time, there will always be a Named Nurse (*see page 30*) to look after your baby.

Doctors

A Consultant Paediatrician will always be in overall charge of your baby's care. He or she usually leads a daily round, and is quite often in the unit during normal working hours.

Senior House Officers are the junior doctors who, along with the nurses, do most of the day-to-day work.

Registrars or Senior Registrars are trainee paediatricians (doctors whose specialist skill is looking after babies and young children) who are working towards becoming Consultants soon.

Medical students do not work in special care baby units — though they may be present as observers and to be taught about the problems of caring for tiny babies. Qualified doctors training in paediatrics will also spend some time in the unit.

You may be asked whether you agree for your baby to be observed/discussed by the Consultant during his rounds with students as part of their medical training.

Specialists

In addition to the above, you may meet a long list of other professionals who are there to help you and your baby, including:

- midwives
- dietitians
- social workers
- chaplains of various denominations
- clinical psychologists
- speech therapists (who have special expertise with feeding problems)
- physiotherapists
- radiographers
- ophthalmologists.

Research Workers

Advanced care for tiny babies is only possible because of years of careful research, much of which has been made possible by charities such as Action Research. This research is still continuing and most neonatal units are involved in some form of clinical trial aimed at improving the care of sick babies.

You may be asked whether you wish your baby to be enrolled in a trial. If so, you will be given a full explanation of what is called for. All research is strictly controlled by each hospital's Ethics Committee. If you do not wish your baby to be involved in a trial, this will not affect the quality of care he receives.

You will always be asked to give consent before a trial starts, and you are free to withdraw your baby from the trial if you change your mind at any point.

Action Research

Since its foundation in 1952, this charity has always been particularly concerned to improve understanding of childhood diseases, and to improve treatment.

Conducting high-quality research is expensive and requires carefully trained specialists. As a medical research charity, Action Research endeavours to provide both the resources and personnel to further its aims. Every year it allocates funds to new research projects, each addressing different medical problems including those of premature babies. To gain the charity's support a project has to pass through a stringent assessment procedure and be approved by a panel of experts.

In addition to funding specific research, Action Research also helps promising newcomers with its Research Training Fellowship scheme. This scheme supports people (usually under the age of 35) who are learning how to perform research projects. This has two major benefits. First of all, throughout their Fellowship they work to unravel some medical mystery, and secondly, having been trained in research they will be in an ideal position to form part of the vital core of tomorrow's medical scientists.

Why Can't We Choose Who Looks after our Baby?

Primary Nurse and Named Nurse

Unfortunately it is not possible to choose your nurse. The care structure is designed to take the needs of each and every baby in the unit into consideration.

Your baby will get all of the attention that he needs. Most units organize this by having a Primary Nurse and a Named Nurse. The Primary Nurse will get to know the baby and his family, while on every shift there will be a Named Nurse who will be in charge of your baby's care throughout that shift.

Your Primary Nurse will also plan the nursing care of your baby in such a way that enables you to join in as much as possible.

Complaints

Being Heard

Under the Patient's Charter, everyone must have an easy route to making a complaint. If you are worried about anything and are not satisfied by the answers you get from doctors or nurses, ask to speak to the Consultant in charge. Failing that, speak to the Service Manager or Director of Services. Their names and titles are usually displayed somewhere in the hospital. If you cannot find their names, ask at the main reception desk.

Chapter Seven

What Can We Do?

One of the hardest things about your baby being in a neonatal unit is that you can easily feel that there is nothing that you can do. The doctors and nurses seem so competent and so much in control. They know just how to handle your baby so that he is caused the least amount of discomfort and they understand all of the monitors and equipment that surrounds your baby's incubator.

In contrast, you can soon feel lost and totally incapable of helping your baby in any way. After the shock of the first few days starts to subside, you need to seek ways of actively joining in with the nursing team and helping wherever possible. The nursing team will be only too pleased to see you joining in. There are many ways in which you can support the hospital staff, and over the weeks while your baby is on the unit you should be able to feel that you are part of this little community.

If your baby was born very early, then over the first few days there may be very little for you to do. But you will be surprised by how quickly you can start to learn about, and help with, his routine care.

Helping the Staff

Being Thoughtful

One of the easiest ways of helping the staff is just to keep in regular contact. This is especially important if you cannot visit your baby for a day or two or have to cancel a visit at short notice. The nurses will give you the telephone number for the unit; remember to take it with you. If you should lose it, Directory Enquiries will be able to give you the main number for the hospital and the switchboard will then put you through.

When you do phone in, ask to speak to the nurse who is looking after your baby. As shifts change throughout the days and weeks, there will be many different nurses looking after your baby. As a result it is easier not to ask for a particular nurse, but instead to ask for 'the nurse looking after baby X'. By doing this you will be put through to the person with the most up-to-date information on your baby. If you phone more than once during a single shift this will also mean that the nurse on duty will know what you have been told already and how much updating you need regarding your baby's recent progress.

Where possible, co-ordinate visits to coincide with things that happen regularly, such as feeding or washing your baby. This has two main advantages. First it means that you will avoid disturbing your baby soon after staff have just got him settled and comfortable. Secondly, and more importantly, it will mean that you have the opportunity to join in with your baby's care. Once you know what to do and feel confident, nursing staff will be very happy to wait for you to arrive, even if you are going to be a few minutes late, so it is good to let them know when you next plan to be in.

As parents, you need to feel able to come in and do things on your own initiative, but do let nurses know what you are intending, and check that it is OK. This will enable you to be part of the team.

Some units prefer parents not to be around during the daily ward round (others actively encourage parent participation). The reason for this is to preserve confidentiality about other babies and their families. The ward rounds do not take very long and are at regular times of day, so it should not be too difficult for you to work around them.

Joining In

Being Part of the Care Team

It is quite normal to feel helpless as experienced staff look after your baby, but do not underestimate the value of your care. Look to the doctors and nurses to show you what you can do. Once you are proficient, this will help them by reducing their workload, and will help you to form a relationship with your baby.

The nurses will help you to do as many tasks for your baby as his condition allows. Certainly, once your baby is ready to go home, you will be able to do everything required.

Don't just stand there feeling helpless, but always ask before trying to do anything.

Being There

The benefits of simply being with your baby are great. It may not seem to you to be as vital as the work the nurses and doctors are doing, but talking to and touching your baby is very important. Do ask a nurse to show you how to touch your baby so that you do not cause him any distress.

Quite often babies will need to be sedated while they are in the neonatal unit. However, even though this means that he cannot respond, your baby will still be able to tell that you are there by the sound of your voice and the feel of your touch. If you regularly spend time with your baby, you will become a source of comfort in the middle of a busy unit.

Washing and Nappy-changing

Washing your baby and changing his nappy may be complex because of all of the tubes and monitors. The nurses will show you how to do this and it will get easier as time passes and fewer and fewer monitors are needed. This will help you to get to know your baby, and give you confidence in handling him.

Supplying Breastmilk/Food for Baby

Once the baby is born, the mother's breasts start to produce milk. This happens as changes occur in her hormone levels. It takes place even though your baby has been born early.

Quite often premature babies cannot suckle as they have not yet developed a proper swallowing reflex. In this case they may need to be fed the milk down a special tube. If your baby is even younger he may not tolerate any milk yet. In this case any milk that you produce can be expressed and frozen until he is ready to take it.

Expressing breastmilk can be made more difficult if the mother becomes anxious or is feeling stressed. The doctors may give you a drug called Maxalon to help stimulate milk production. The National Childbirth Trust (NCT) have a great many guides and give sensible tips and advice on using breast pumps. Their address is included at the end of this book.

Breastmilk is an excellent source of nutrients for babies. In addition to this, during the first few days after birth the milk (known at this point as colostrum) contains molecules of protein that help to give your baby a strong defence against infections. If you had not planned to breastfeed your baby, the hospital may be able to supply breastmilk from a milk-bank.

Staff will also train you to use any special feeding equipment.

How Should We Hold our Baby?

A Calming Cuddle

Holding a baby is a strong way of forming an emotional bond with him. Over the first few days or maybe even weeks, your baby will be so fragile that even gently picking him up will cause him pain and possibly even damage. However, there will come a time when your baby is strong enough for you to lift him up and cuddle him as he lays naked on your chest. This is called skin-to-skin contact, or 'kangaroo care'.

The idea of looking after tiny babies by keeping them warm lying between their mothers' breasts was first put into practice in the South American country of Colombia. There, doctors short of facilities developed a system of care that dispensed with incubators and artificial feeds and taught mothers how to care for their babies at home. While the technique was remarkably successful, it is not as good as the full intensive care that a well-equipped neonatal unit can supply. However, combined with modern medicine the practice has many benefits and has started to be used in many units. Nursing staff now encourage parents to lift their baby out of the incubator and lay him on their chests, tucked underneath their shirts, with a blanket over the top.

Among the advantages of 'kangaroo care' is the fact that it is a very enjoyable experience for you to be able to cuddle your baby and feel his skin against your own. This will be the first time you have had such intimate contact with him.

When introducing this practice was first put forward, some medical staff were worried about the idea of removing babies from the safety of their incubators. Therefore, clinical trials were conducted to ensure that the practice was safe. Some of the babies included in the trials even had chronic lung disease and needed a ventilator to help them breathe. The results were very positive:

- Women giving skin-to-skin care found that their milk production improved. During skin-to-skin sessions, many women reported feeling their nipples tingling and milk swelling up in their breasts. This enabled them to express milk for six weeks longer than women who had not had skin-to-skin contact with their baby.
- Babies who had been held against their parents' chests cried significantly less at six months of age. This suggests that they were greatly comforted by the contact with their parents.
- While they were lying on their parents' chests, babies had fewer episodes of apnoea (stopping breathing). Quite possibly, lying in a slightly more upright position helps them breathe more regularly.
- During skin-to-skin contact, babies had slightly higher heart rates.
- In the comfort of their parent's gentle embrace, babies spent more time in deep sleep, which is thought to be good for brain development, and indicates that they were relaxed.
- Throughout a skin-to-skin session babies were found to have more oxygen in their blood. This indicates that they were calm and able to breathe well. It is of particular advantage to babies with damaged lungs.

One of the main anxieties that people have about removing a baby from the protection of an incubator is that it will cause him to cool down. However, the trials showed that:

1. if the baby wears a little cap
2. is kept sprawled against his parent's skin
3. and a blanket is placed over the top of the baby and mother

then during the skin-to-skin sessions his body temperature will neither rise nor fall.

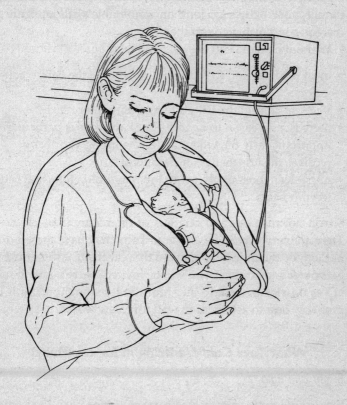

*"I love the feel of him against my skin.
I can even feel him breathing."*

What Clothes Can We Bring in for our Baby?

Don't Dress Up

At first, you may not be allowed to dress your baby. Even though your baby may look uncomfortable without clothes, there is good reason for this.

Without clothes...

- most medical staff find it easier to observe the baby's condition
- staff can control the baby's temperature more easily
- there is less reason to handle your baby; this is particularly important early on, when the less handling your baby receives the less distress he is caused
- nurses can more easily get to tubes and monitors attached to your baby.

So, do not rush out and buy lots of premature baby clothes. They are very expensive and your baby may have grown out of them by the time he is allowed to wear them. As your baby gets older and stronger you will be invited to dress him. If relatives or friends want to buy him clothes straight away, it is probably best to ask them to wait for a few weeks.

What Toys Can We Bring in for our Baby?

Bright and Bold

Even quite premature babies can see things once they have reached 30 weeks of development.

The best toys have clear outlines and are made of bold black-and-white patterned material. Babies can also see very bold colours, but will have difficulty seeing any object made of pastel-coloured material. Bold reds and oranges are best at first.

It is a great idea to encourage brothers and sisters to draw some bold pictures to decorate the inside of your baby's incubator. A photograph of your family is a nice touch, identifying as it does the baby as a member of your family.

Only bring one or two toys — remember that staff still need to be able to see your baby, and after all, they are there to look after him, not his toys! Labelling them in some way will help to ensure that they do not get lost.

Medical Challenges

Specialized intensive care for premature babies continues to improve. Looking after premature babies has developed into a high technology service. We now understand many of the challenges that a premature baby faces as he fights for life. Doctors have developed equipment and treatments that target each challenge, supporting premature babies while they continue to develop and grow.

Challenge 1 — Breathing

Premature babies sometimes have great problems breathing. Most will need some help, at least to start with. Such assistance may be given either by increasing the amount of oxygen that is available or by artificially ventilating his lungs.

Four Reasons for Poor Lung Function

No Surfactant

The most common reason for babies needing ventilatory support is that their lungs are too immature to produce a substance called *surfactant*. This substance has similar properties to washing-up liquid. It is normally produced in cells inside lungs and spreads across the surface of the airways. As it coats the surface, it changes the surface tension and makes sure that the airways stay open, allowing air to enter.

Lack of surfactant can be treated in most cases by putting

an artificial form of it into the baby's lungs. This artificial surfactant is often given in two doses on the day of birth. Premature babies start to produce their own surfactant a few days after birth, so doctors only need to help them through the first few days.

Physically Small Lungs

Premature babies are very small. While their lungs have developed a long way, they still have very small airways. This makes it difficult for air to move in and out, and breathing can be hard work. If they have to work too hard, the muscles that organize breathing will tire and stop working. Also, any small obstructions easily block airways, making sections of their lungs ineffective. Nurses regularly check that there is no mucus blocking air passages. They may also help babies by increasing the amount of oxygen in the air they are breathing.

An Immature Control System

Breathing is controlled by our brains. We do not have to think about it, it just looks after itself. Some premature babies are born before this control mechanism is sufficiently developed. Doctors call this Apnoea of Prematurity (apnoea is Greek for 'no breathing').

In this case a machine can breathe for them while their brains have time to complete their own control systems.

Infection

Pneumonia can be a severe problem in premature babies. Such an infection causes mucus to collect in the lungs. This mucus blocks the tubes and prevents oxygen getting deep inside the lungs. Pneumonia is usually treated with antibiotics, but in the mean time the baby may need help with his breathing.

Breathing Equipment

Ventilators

Ventilators perform a very simple job. They carefully inflate the baby's lungs, passing oxygen in, and then allow the lungs to deflate so that carbon dioxide can be removed. Having said that, they are extremely expensive pieces of equipment because they have complex control and safety systems.

A ventilator feeds oxygen and air to a baby via a tube in his windpipe (trachea). This tube will either pass through his mouth or down his nose, and will often be held in place by tying it to a bonnet or hat.

Some baby units use negative pressure ventilation. This involves putting the baby in a large, transparent box that covers him from the neck down (that is, his head is exposed through a seal at one end of the box). The pressure in the box is reduced, so lessening the pressure on the baby's chest. As a result it is easier to help him to breathe.

Drugs to Help

While babies are being ventilated, they need to be kept calm and prevented from moving excessively. The gentlest way of doing this is to sedate them. This also lessens the discomfort they might otherwise feel as a result of all the pipes and tubes. While babies are sedated, extra fluids may collect in their bodies. As a result they may appear to be slightly puffy and swollen. This will disappear once sedation is no longer required.

In some hospitals, doctors give babies corticosteroids to help their lungs develop. These steroids are very different from the anabolic steroids made infamous in the world of sport.

By the time they leave the baby unit, many babies will have been given more than one course of antibiotics. These are often needed to help clear up chest infections.

Suction

Mucus and fluid are frequently sucked out of the baby's mouth. It is important to prevent this sliding down into his lungs, where it could cause a blockage or lead to an infection.

Nasal Prongs

Some babies can breathe on their own, but need a little help to get enough oxygen to their lungs. The amount of oxygen that they take in with each breath can be increased using nasal prongs. Usually made of silicone rubber tubes, they are attached to a supply of oxygen. This oxygen enriches the air that the baby is breathing and so increases the amount that gets into his lungs. One advantage of nasal oxygen therapy is that babies can easily be cuddled and fed out of their cots or incubators, while continuing to receive the necessary oxygen.

Head Box

A less intrusive method of increasing oxygen is to put a Perspex box over the baby's head and feed a mixture of oxygen and air into it. The amount of oxygen given is regulated to achieve minute-by-minute control of the amount of oxygen in the baby's blood.

Apnoea Alarms

When a baby comes off a ventilator it can take a number of days or weeks before he becomes used to breathing on his own. Such babies have a tendency to stop breathing (a condition known as apnoea); they then need to be aroused so that they start to breathe again.

A variety of different alarms can be used to monitor the baby's breathing. They are all known as apnoea alarms. Some electrically monitor chest movement, others monitor the physical movement of breathing. Whatever they measure, an alarm will sound if the baby stops breathing or if the alarm becomes disconnected.

Chronic Lung Disease

Even using modern ventilators, a baby's lungs may become damaged in the course of any kind of treatment to help him to breathe. This is particularly the case if high pressures are necessary. The high levels of oxygen that are needed can also damage the delicate lining of the lungs, as can any underlying disease being treated.

Doctors will always use the minimum amount of ventilation and the lowest levels of oxygen that they can. However, if they have to work hard ventilating lungs in the first few days there is some risk that the baby may have problems with his lungs as a result. These problems may persist throughout childhood, although they will slowly improve as he grows up.

Some babies will only need oxygen for the first week or so, but others will need it for the first few months after birth. Doctors say that a baby has 'chronic lung disease' if he needs additional oxygen or ventilation for more than 28 days. (Some doctors may call this Bronchopulmonary Dysplasia, or BPD.)

Challenge 2 — Keeping Warm

Of all challenges, keeping warm is one of the most urgent. In a special care unit, it is also one that is most easily solved. To start with, the temperature of the whole unit is kept very warm. In addition, babies will either be placed in an incubator or under a radiant heater.

Premature babies get cold incredibly easily. This is because:

- they are born with very little fat underneath their skin, which means that they have little natural insulation
- they have few reserves of energy that can be burned to produce heat
- full-term babies and children have a tissue called brown fat, which generates heat. This is absent in premature babies.

They are also so small that they lose heat very easily. As a result they rely to a great extent on getting heat from their surroundings.

If premature babies start to get cold, they use some of their energy supply to generate heat. This means that the energy cannot be used to help them develop and grow. Most premature babies can only just take in enough food to grow, so wasting energy on keeping warm at best slows growth, and at worst can be very damaging.

Incubators

The Perspex Box

An incubator is basically a simple plastic box, but once fitted with monitoring equipment it becomes a very sophisticated piece of equipment.

Most are double-glazed, being made from two sheets of Perspex. This helps to keep the temperature inside the incubator at a constant level, and also allows for the temperature to be hotter inside the incubator than outside it. The double glazing also reduces the amount of noise that can get through, which might otherwise disturb the baby.

Electronically controlled systems monitor the temperature inside each incubator and also the temperature of the baby. They aim to keep his temperature constant, and sound an alarm if it changes too much. Other systems regulate the amount of oxygen and the humidity in the incubator. Again, alarms sound if either of these changes.

Very small babies may need an additional heat shield placed over them.

Open-air Incubators

Radiant Heaters

Radiant heaters are particularly useful for babies who need a lot of medical help. As the baby is not contained in an incubator, doctors and nurses can get to him more easily to provide any treatment he may need.

Babies lie naked under the heater, which is connected to a machine that measures the baby's temperature and controls how much heat is given out. If his temperature changes, an alarm sounds to alert staff.

How Heat Is Lost

Convection

In convection, heat is lost to the air surrounding the baby. If the air temperature is low, or if the baby is in a draught, then losses due to convection can be great.

Radiation

This radiation has nothing to do with radioactivity! Instead it refers to the way that a baby will lose heat to any nearby object that is cooler than he is. This will happen even if the air temperature is warm. For this reason, babies should not be kept near a cold window, even if the room is warm. Radiant heaters reverse this process by placing a warm surface near the baby. This means that heat will be transferred from the warm surface to the baby.

Evaporation

When water evaporates from a surface, that surface gets colder. You can feel this when you get out of a swimming pool: you immediately feel cold as the water evaporates, even if you emerge into sunshine on a hot day.

One way nurses minimize evaporation is by not washing babies. Even if you use warm water, the water has to be dried off. The process of drying causes a lot of heat to be lost from the baby's skin.

There are no problems in leaving a baby unwashed. He may have bits of dried blood and be covered in a white, greasy, cheese-like substance called vernix, but neither carries infections nor harms him if left on. In fact, the vernix offers a bit of protection to the baby's skin as well as helping to insulate against heat loss.

Also, a premature baby's skin is terribly fragile for the first few days. Some babies will bruise even when little sensors are placed on them. Washing a baby may cause more damage through bruising.

Conduction

In conduction, babies lose heat if they lie on a cold surface. Once your baby is in a baby unit, this is very rarely a problem.

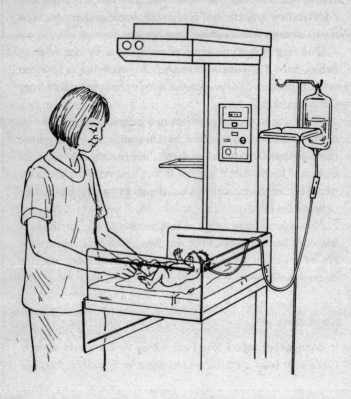

One style of incubator equipped with an overhead radiant heater.

Challenge 3 — Feeding

Most babies are not able to suck well enough to take adequate nourishment until they are the equivalent of 32 — 36 weeks old. Until they can suck reliably, without using up too much energy, they need food to be supplied artificially.

If a baby's gut is sufficiently developed, milk can be passed directly into his stomach using a special feeding tube. However, quite often a baby's stomach and gut are not capable of processing enough food, so additional nutrients are given to the baby using an intravenous drip. Doctors are now capable of supplying the whole of a baby's nutrient requirement by drip. However, they may also try to introduce a little milk into his stomach, as even a teaspoonful will encourage the digestive system to grow and develop properly. If the milk used is breastmilk, it will also protect the baby from many different diseases.

Jejunal Feeding

Sometimes doctors may choose to pass a tube directly into the small intestine, or jejunum. This has the advantage of preventing the baby from bringing food up into his lungs while he is being ventilated.

Blood Tests

Doctors obtain a lot of information about a baby's health from blood samples. While a baby is being artificially fed it is very important to check that his liver is working properly, and that there is the right balance of different substances (such as glucose and potassium) in his bloodstream. Doctors and nurses will frequently sample your baby's blood to check that everything is under control.

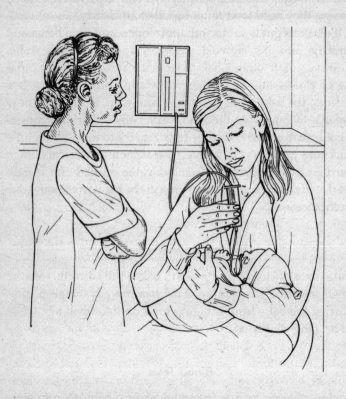

*Nurses will teach you how to feed your baby, helping you
to be involved in looking after your baby.*

Challenge 4 — Blood

The smallest premature baby may have as little as 40 millilitres (ml) of blood. Every day while he is in the neonatal unit, doctors will need to take up to 5 ml of blood for different measurements. The baby will not be able to make up this amount of blood each day, so doctors replace it using blood transfusions.

Blood Transfusions

The great advantage of blood transfusions is that they do not use any of the baby's energy. New blood is simply supplied.

Donors who give blood for use in baby units are rigorously screened to ensure that their blood is not infected with CMV (Cytomegalovirus, a virus which can cause great damage to premature babies), hepatitis B virus (which causes liver damage), or HIV (the virus that causes AIDS).

Babies may be given either whole blood or individual constituents of blood such as plasma and platelets.

Challenge 5 — Jaundice

A baby's skin and eyes sometimes turn yellow a few days after birth. This is due to the accumulation of bilirubin in his blood. Bilirubin is a material that is released when old blood cells are broken down. It is normally removed by the liver. However, in many premature babies their livers are immature and cannot cope. If bilirubin accumulates in large amounts it may cause brain damage.

Phototherapy

Unlike many other problems, jaundice is usually easily solved. The baby is simply undressed and placed under a strong source of blue light, or on a special blanket that emits blue light. The light causes the bilirubin molecules to change shape. The newly shaped molecules are now easily removed from his body.

Unlike ultraviolet light, this blue light is totally harmless to his skin, but because it is so strong it must be kept out of his eyes by the use of a mask or coloured Perspex shade.

Exchange Transfusions

In some cases, phototherapy alone does not remove the bilirubin quickly. A small number of babies still need what are known as *exchange blood transfusions*. This is where some of the baby's blood is removed and replaced with donated blood, thus rapidly clearing bilirubin from the baby.

Challenge 6 — Surgery

There are many different conditions that may need to be treated by surgery. If your baby needs an operation, then this should not be delayed. A doctor will carefully explain why an operation may be needed and ask for permission before carrying it out. Although doctors used to be very worried about anaesthetizing premature babies, new methods make this quite safe and do not expose babies to unnecessary risks.

Facing your Feelings

Most parents whose baby arrives many weeks early are devastated and suffer a pronounced form of loss. They feel as if they have been thrown head-long into a world of medicine, technology and science that is far removed from everyday life, and consequently one that is very frightening. Caught up in a crisis, parents face a series of unexpected events for which they have been given little or no preparation. The birth itself will have seemed all the more traumatic as the mother and father feel totally out of control and vulnerable.

Once the delivery is over, it can be quite a shock seeing your tiny baby and what looks like a mass of tubes and high-tech equipment. If your baby needs a ventilator to help him breathe you will hardly be able to see his face, particularly if he is also wearing a bonnet to keep his head warm.

Even though you are surrounded by people who are paid to look after you, parents can feel very alone and isolated. This perception is then compounded as, not knowing how to cope, many friends and family either avoid you or ask questions that you may not want to think about. Even if you want to, you may not know how to answer them.

You may feel a failure: 'After all, everybody else seems to manage all right.'

You will definitely feel disappointed: 'If only our baby was well...'

You will have a sense of grief as your dreams seem to fade: 'All we wanted was a healthy baby.'

> You have lost many things:
>
> * You hoped for a strong, healthy baby
>   – instead your baby is very weak.
> * You were preparing yourself for a normal birth
>   – instead you had an emergency delivery.
> * You were looking forward to an intimate time at home with your baby
>   – instead your baby is in hospital.
> * you were expecting to take your baby home and show him off proudly to everyone
>   – instead you may not even be able to find the words to tell others about him.

Fear

All sorts of possibilities will flash through your mind, leaving you frightened and confused:

* Will our baby die?
* Will our baby be handicapped?
* How will we cope?
* What happens now?

The shock of a premature birth will leave you fearful and tearful as you try to make sense of the situation over the first few days. No amount of people telling you not to worry makes any difference — you are worried.

On top of this, the mother may still be affected by the physical trauma of the birth. She may have to go by wheelchair everywhere for the first day or two, which introduces problems of its own — it's easy to feel as if you are in the way when confined to a chair, and very difficult to do anything to help yourself – much less anyone else.

As if this were not enough, some of the medication that the mother has been given may still cloud her mind. This can make her extremely tired and may make it difficult for her to concentrate for more than a few minutes at a time.

Guilt

Is It my Fault?

It is very easy for your disappointment to spill over into feelings of guilt. Some women start to feel guilty that they did not carry their baby to term, that they did not have a normal labour and are not able to look after their baby.

However real, the fact is that there is no foundation to these feelings. It is not your fault; in the vast majority of cases it isn't anybody's fault.

If you have these feelings, talk to your midwife or nurse — you are not alone. Find out how other people have coped with these feelings. If they cannot help you themselves, they will introduce you to someone who can tell you how other families have coped, put you in touch with a support group and, if necessary, introduce you to an experienced psychologist, social worker or counsellor.

Where Do I Start?

Take Time to Face your Feelings

When you first arrived in the baby unit you probably experienced a sense of pure shock — so much activity, unusual noises and alarms, doctors and nurses actively getting on with their work.

Remember that the nurses are there to help you, as well as your baby. They are very good at making parents feel safe. However, it may take many days before you will be able to look around the baby unit and notice the people, rather than the machines.

Your baby is in the best place that he could be.

Coping with Questions

Retire But Do Not Hide

You need to keep family and friends informed so that they can help you, but you may feel unable to cope with answering the same questions each time another person phones.

Some people try to avoid this by taking the phone off the hook or staying away from home. Neither of these options is particularly practical in the long term.

The Telephone

Many telephones can now be diverted. Ask a friend or relative if he or she would mind answering questions, and divert your phone to his or her line when you feel that you need a break. This way friends can find out how you and your baby are getting on without always disturbing you.

Alternatively, you could regularly update the message on an answerphone. Friends could then ring for information and you could 'screen' their calls — that is, listen to who is calling before deciding to pick up the phone.

Friends can help by giving various kinds of practical support, such as:

- bringing meals round
- giving lifts to and from hospital
- taking you to the station if you need a train
- helping to care for any older children that you may have
- shutting up when you do not want to talk.

Coping at Work

This will take a number of days, maybe even weeks.

Fathers may have to go back to work very soon after the birth, often before there has been time for the situation to sink in. Before you return to work, take a moment to consider how you will answer any questions. If you are busy at work you may need to block the problem out of your mind for a few hours.

It may help to practise the phrases you plan to use before you go in to work. Answers that avoid getting into complicated explanations include:

'We're just taking it one day at a time.'

'I can't bear to think about it at the moment — sorry.'

'I really don't know all the answers myself at the moment.'

You could tell one friend at work a little more about the situation, and then tell everyone else to ask him or her.

This can also work well at home, where you could tell one friend or relative and direct all other people to him or her for information.

Support from Other Parents in the Unit

Be considerate of other parents in the unit.

Remember, you do not like people pestering you for details about how your baby is getting on.

But:

- do ask how they are
- do go for a drink in small groups — a good time to relax and discuss coping strategies. Some units run regular parents' meetings which can be useful for swapping ideas.

Bonding

The Importance of Being a Parent

A major fear of any parent is that the baby will start to become more attached to the doctors and nurses than to his parents. You may start to believe that, because so much is carried out by other people, your input is of little value. More importantly, you may worry that you are not finding it easy to bond and form a strong relationship with your baby right from the start.

NOTE: bonding is no less strong between parents and babies who have been in a neonatal unit than between parents and their full-term babies who go straight home.

> **As your baby's parents you are unique.**
> **You have a vital role to play and no one can**
> **replace you.**

What Is Unique about Being A Parent?

Nurses change every shift — parents do not change.

Nursing staff are very dedicated people, but they are also doing a job and working on shifts. Each day your baby will be cared for by many different nurses and doctors, but as parents you offer the most consistent loving attention, touch and communication.

How Can I Let my Baby Know I'm Here?

Talking and Touching

Nursing staff will encourage as much contact as possible between parents and their baby. They will show you many things that you can do. Your baby will soon learn that you are a source of kindness and comfort.

- Parents do gentle things to their baby.
- Nurses do things that are medically required — some of which may be uncomfortable or even slightly painful.
- Your baby may be able to recognize his parents' gentle touch compared to the doctors' and nurses' heavier hands.

Keep talking — your baby can hear your voices even if some of the drugs he has been given prevent him showing any response.

- Parents can sit on either side of his cot and talk to each other.
- Talk about anything, everything.
- Keep your voices calm.
- Your baby knows his parents' voices, so hearing them is reassuring.

Touch Is Important

You know how much you like to be held gently by someone who loves you — well, so does your baby.

- Reach out and touch — as your baby grows, there will be different ways to touch your baby — allow a nurse to demonstrate and show you what is best.
- Often it is possible to hold the baby on your lap.
- You may be allowed to place him on your chest under your shirt — this also keeps him warm, and the skin-to-skin contact is pleasant and beneficial to your baby and to you.

*Bringing older children for a visit unites the family
and helps them to understand what is happening.*

Going Home Empty-handed

Home Alone

Possibly one of the most traumatic days is the one when you leave hospital but your baby stays. Mothers should try not to go home on their own — they will be exhausted after the previous weeks' activities (particularly if your baby was delivered by a caesarean section) and extremely emotional. Try to give staff at the hospital telephone numbers where they can contact you; this will help to make you feel less isolated and more involved.

Looking after the Rest of your Family

Coping with Other Children

Try to find someone who can look after other children for at least some of your visits, so that both parents can visit together. Occasionally this may be important if you have a planned meeting with a member of the hospital staff.

At weekends, or after school, take brothers and sisters with you, but remember that they may get bored if visits are too long with little or nothing to occupy them.

The problems tend to start to get worse if the new baby stays more than a few weeks. At this point the whole family is likely to be feeling strained, as older children start to miss parental attention.

Take time to explain to any older children just what is going on — they will realize how worried you are. At the same time they need reassurance about how much mum and dad love them. Explain that right now you all need each other's support.

The arrival of any younger brother or sister can be a source of jealousy, but a premature baby demands so much time and attention that this may be particularly marked.

Depression

When Blues Seem Black

Many women suffer from a mild depression called 'the baby blues'. This lasts only a few days and will go away without any need for medical assistance.

A more serious form is called post-natal depression. It affects about 1 in 10 mothers and may last for weeks. Tell one of the staff if you are feeling seriously depressed; he or she will help you find specialist care and treatment.

These forms of depression are not a statement about your character. They may be due to hormone changes that accompany the end of pregnancy and the stress of having a small or sick baby in hospital. Do not feel ashamed if you feel tearful, low and unable to cope. Tell one of the staff if you are feeling seriously depressed or if you notice that your behaviour is very different to normal. He or she will be able to refer you to someone who can help.

Many units set up support groups, often holding weekly meetings run by trained staff. Parents who have been through a similar situation in the past are also involved in these groups, adding greatly to the depth of experience and helping to support new, uninitiated parents.

Conflicting Information

Whom Should We Ask?

Because everything is so new to you and you are in a state of shock, the same information given by different people may seem different. If you are depressed you are likely to have to ask the same questions a number of times — do not worry about this.

The body is a wonderfully complex machine, and doctors have equally complicated ways of treating its problems. Do not be surprised if you find it difficult to understand some of their procedures and explanations.

There are some simple things to do that will help:

- Always try to get your information from the same person.
- Find the member of staff whom you can understand most easily.
- Have your baby's Named Nurse sit in with you when a doctor is explaining anything — then you can ask him or her questions about what the doctor said as often as you need.

What if our Baby Should Die?

A Death in the Family

Although all parents worry about their baby dying, most babies in neonatal units do survive and grow up normally.

The thought of the death of any baby is absolutely appalling — for a baby to die so young seems particularly horrific and unfair.

But take a moment to look at it from the baby's point of view:

- You have given him your love and your care.
- He will always be a member of your family — an important member.
- He has never been aware of any great suffering or hardship, and was cared for every moment of his short life.

Do not worry about getting 'too involved' with your baby. In any case it can be difficult to avoid, as you are likely to see your baby as a real person from early in the pregnancy, a perception that is often reinforced with the first scan (for fathers as well as mothers). Becoming attached to your baby is very normal and in the long term it is good for everyone. It often helps you to avoid suffering from guilt later.

Do not underestimate how long it will take you to recover from the loss of your baby. He may have only had a short life, but even if you tried to distance yourself from the situation you will have been emotionally very involved.

If your baby does die, the hospital will help you to make arrangements.

- Where possible, but only if you desire, you will be there when your baby dies.
- You will be encouraged to wash and dress your baby — this helps you to take comfort later from the fact that you cared for your baby right up to the end.

Neonatal units have special rooms for parents and other family members who want some private time alone with the baby. Nurses will stay with the family or leave them to be on their own, whichever the family wishes. It may be quite some time before you want to part with your baby. The hospital will lend you a camera if you do not have one with you. As well as taking a last photo of your baby, you may also want to keep a small lock of his hair, or your baby's name band.

Your baby will then be laid in a non-denominational chapel of rest, where you and your family can spend as long as you feel you need.

If you gave birth to more than one baby (twins, triplets, or maybe even quadruplets) and one baby dies, you may wish to delay the funeral until you know that the others are safe. This is perfectly possible, and once again the hospital will make all of the necessary arrangements.

The staff will also help you to find counsellors to speak with. A list of organizations that assist in counselling is provided at the back of this book.

What about my Next Pregnancy?

Will It End Early?

Having had one premature baby, many parents are justifiably anxious to know what is likely to happen when they are ready to have another at some point in the future. Various questions need addressing: Are there things we can do to increase the chances of having a normal pregnancy? Is there any medical help that would be an advantage?

The reasons for a premature birth vary greatly, and as was explained earlier in the book many premature births occur for no apparent reason. To know what is likely to happen to you, if you decide to have another baby you should see an Obstetrician who specializes in looking after women with premature babies.

During the time that your baby is in the neonatal unit, you may have had a chance to speak to a Consultant Obstetrician. He or she will be able to discuss your individual circumstances and give you individual advice. If this has not happened, then ask for an appointment to see an Obstetrician. Your GP will be able to tell you the best way to do this.

There are, however, some general points that are worth considering:

- Two-thirds of women who have a premature baby do not have any problems with any subsequent pregnancy. It is by no means an automatic assumption that just because one baby came early, any others will follow suit.
- Wherever possible, avoid placing yourself in a stressful situation during your next pregnancy. This is often easier said than done, and may mean that you need to consider stopping work for the whole of your pregnancy.
- As many premature births are thought to be caused by an infection, it is well worth seeing your doctor as soon as you know you are pregnant again. He or she will be able

to see whether there are any signs of an infection, and will give you antibiotics if there is any cause for concern.

- For the duration of your pregnancy it is worth avoiding any strenuous activity or sport. Gentle exercise can help you keep fit, but don't go mad!
- Some people believe that chemicals (prostaglandins) found in a man's semen can trigger labour. While this is only a theory, if you want to take every precaution it is probably worth using a condom when making love while you are pregnant.

None of these measures can guarantee a trouble-free pregnancy next time round, but every little helps.

Going Home – The Second Shock

It may seem difficult to believe, but from the moment your baby was admitted to the unit staff have been preparing and planning for the day you take him home. Over the weeks you will start to look forward to having your baby at home. However, when you are eventually told that your baby is well enough to go home, it may be a moment of concern and even shock.

When Will our Baby Be Ready to Come Home?

A Stable Condition

Before your baby goes home, he will need to have grown and matured enough to have solved most of his ongoing medical problems. It is usually feeding that holds babies back. Your baby will need to be able to feed, by either breast or bottle, and to keep putting on weight. Having said this, there is usually no set target weight to be reached before doctors let your baby go.

Some babies may be discharged from hospital with special needs. If this is the case, these needs, and how they will be met, will be discussed fully with you. Your health visitor and sometimes your community nurse will also help you at home.

Most areas of Britain are now covered by specialized neonatal outreach teams or a community-based paediatric home care team. A member of these teams will get to know you and your family so that they are in the best position to help you.

The needs of your whole family will be taken into consideration in deciding the best time for you to take your baby home.

When you do go home, please send a photo of your baby to the unit. This will be put up on a board and is a great encouragement to parents who are just arriving in the unit.

What Is the Relationship between my Local GP, Health Visitor and Hospital Unit?

A New Band of Helpers

When your baby is discharged from hospital, a letter will be sent to your GP. This will give him or her all of the medical information he or she needs to look after your baby well in future.

Your local health visitor will have been contacted when your baby was born, and will have been following his progress in hospital. Whenever possible, a health visitor will visit your home before the baby joins you, helping you to plan ahead and be ready to bring him home. You may also see your health visitor in the baby unit.

If your baby has any special needs when he is discharged, then these will be discussed with your GP so that he or she is fully aware of any problems. In short, everything possible is done to try to ensure a smooth transition of care from hospital to home.

At last, you can go home.

Whom Can I Phone for Advice?

Help Is at Hand

If your baby is unwell once he is at home, you will need to get some advice. Do not wait too long, as it is important to catch any problem early. There are three different people whom you can contact: your GP, Health Visitor, or the Baby Unit.

GP

If you are worried that your baby is unwell, phone your GP. You may be able to discuss the problem over the phone, or to make an appointment for that day. Now that your baby is out of hospital you should always try to contact your own doctor first.

Health Visitor

Your health visitor is there to help you. She can be contacted throughout the day and will often be able to give you all the advice that you need — particularly about feeding, daily routines and development.

Baby Unit

If you are stuck and cannot contact your GP or health visitor, then phone the neonatal unit. They will happily talk to you. However, you need to develop a relationship with your local GP and health visitor, so always try them first.

If you think that it is an emergency, take your baby to a hospital Accident and Emergency Department.

Unless you have some prior arrangement, do not take your baby back to the baby unit. Once he has been discharged and taken home, it is very unlikely that he will be readmitted to the baby unit. If for any reason he has to be readmitted to hospital, he will be nursed in a children's ward. It would be very unsafe for other babies in the unit if a baby who may have picked up germs from outside were brought in.

What Temperature Should We Keep our Home?

Not a Hot House

You want to aim to keep the room that your baby is in at around 65°F (18°C). Keeping the room either too hot or too cold can be dangerous. By the time your baby is allowed home he will have matured to the point where he can control his temperature as well as any baby born at full term.

Your house should not be as warm as the neonatal unit. In the unit, many of the babies wear no clothes, so the temperature has to be hot. At home your baby will be wearing clothes, and so will prefer a slightly cooler room.

In winter you may need to keep the baby's room slightly warmer than the rest of the house. However, the main danger is over-heating. Sometimes parents are so anxious not to let their baby get cold that they heat the room and pile on many blankets. This could result in the baby over-heating, which is dangerous.

A few thin layers of bedding are better than one large blanket folded up, as layers can be added or taken away easily. Be careful not to wrap your baby tightly in bedclothes, because then he will not be able to kick them off if he gets too hot. Also, do not place his cot near a radiator. Ask your health visitor if you are unsure about just what is necessary to keep your baby at the right temperature.

Your baby's hands and feet often feel quite cold, but this is not a good indication of his temperature. Check your baby's temperature by placing the palm of your hand on the back of his neck or on his tummy. If the baby seems hot or moist, remove a blanket. If he seems unwell and has a high temperature, contact your GP.

If you think that your baby is too cold, warm him gently by holding him next to your body and covering him with a blanket.

Where Should our Baby Sleep?

Sweet Dreams

Most parents feel happier if their baby sleeps in the same room with them for the first few months. However, it is much safer for your baby to be in his own cot, and not in your bed.

You may, however, be surprised at first just how noisy your baby is while he sleeps. Many parents find this very distracting and have difficulty sleeping with their baby in the same room. Other parents feel that their baby needs to get used to sleeping in a room on his own, and so provide a second bedroom from the start — though this is unusual if the baby was born prematurely.

Parents are now advised by the Department of Health to place their baby on his back when putting him down to sleep. However, for medical reasons your doctor may suggest something different. Do ask questions if you are unsure.

What Are the Signs of Distress?

Warning Signs

One of the most obvious signs of distress is crying. However, crying is the way that babies try to tell you everything, so not every cry is a sign of distress. Quite quickly you will learn to tell when a cry means 'I need feeding' or 'I need a new nappy.' Sometimes the cry may sound very different, and this could indicate that something is not quite right. Most doctors would prefer to see your baby before he has got really unwell, as it will be easier to treat him at this stage. There is nothing to be lost by seeking advice early.

There are other less obvious signs. He may:

- seem unusually listless and limp
- refuse feeds
- feel too hot
- keep vomiting or producing greenish vomit
- have frequent diarrhoea
- have difficulty breathing
- show signs of discomfort when you move or touch him.

All of these indicate that something is not quite right and that you should contact your doctor.

What Should We Feed our Baby?

The Good Food Guide

If you would like to breastfeed your baby, discuss it with your midwife or nursing staff soon after your baby is born, and establish a feeding pattern while he is still in hospital. Many women find this works out well, but it is often quite difficult at first.

Occasionally a baby may need a special formula feed, in which case staff on the baby unit will tell parents what is needed and where they can get it. Your health visitor will give you ongoing advice about how to increase the amount of milk that your baby has as he grows. Vitamin and iron supplements may be prescribed, depending on the type of feeding and on your baby's particular needs.

Weaning

Different people feel that there are different times at which to start to wean a baby. Ask the neonatal staff or your health visitor when they think that it would be appropriate for you to start weaning. On the whole, most premature babies are ready to begin weaning by the time they are three to six months past their due date. There is no need to rush weaning. It is best to introduce your baby to small amounts of different solid foods gradually, one at a time, and make sure he is happy with each new type before moving on to introduce another.

You may start by feeding your baby using a nasogastric tube as well as a bottle or your breast. However, by the time you go home the tube should be unnecessary.

What Precautions Are Necessary When Taking our Baby Out?

Keeping Healthy

You need to start to normalize your life as soon as possible, so be careful not to get into the habit of staying stuck indoors because you are afraid to venture out of the house. However, when you do go shopping, initially try to choose a time when there will be fewer people. This will minimize the risk of your baby coming into contact with germs.

Babies that have been prematurely born are particularly prone to respiratory diseases. If you can reduce the risks of coming into contact with diseases in the early days, especially during the winter, then your baby will progress more quickly. In practice this can be particularly difficult if there are older brothers or sisters at home. Do not worry, just do your best. If you are seeing your health visitor regularly at home, it is probably worth avoiding 'well baby clinics' at first, as there will be many children there who are carrying respiratory viruses and childhood illnesses.

Always avoid taking your baby into smoky areas. In fact, it is strongly advised that no one smokes anywhere in the house, especially if the baby has had lung problems.

Oxygen Treatment at Home

Some premature babies are sent home while they still need oxygen to help them overcome lung disease. They may need it for a few weeks, or for several months. The great advantage is, of course, that your baby is home. Babies thrive more successfully at home. They grow better, they do not pick up as many infections, they feed better and they are with their families.

A nurse will teach you how to use the equipment and arrange for it to be installed in your home. You will either use cylinders or a special oxygen concentrator. Small portable cylinders are also available so that you can take your baby with you when you go out.

Medication for your Baby

Always Ask If You Are Unsure

Any medication recommended for newborn babies will be safe for your baby once you are at home. Follow the guidelines accurately, and use the dose indicated for a newly born full-term baby, not for one that is a few months old.

Make sure that you understand what you need to do with any medication that you have been given by the hospital. If in doubt, contact your local GP. Also, when you run out and need a repeat prescription, go to your GP, not back to the hospital.

Returning for Check-ups

Keeping Appointments

It is normal for a baby to have a follow-up appointment in the Out-patients Clinic. This gives you the chance to discuss any problems that you might have, and for the hospital to monitor your baby's progress. Your first appointment is normally within a few weeks of discharge; it is very important both for you and for your baby that you attend.

Your baby may, if necessary, be taken back to the hospital for special checks.

Is There Any Financial Help Available?

Money Matters

There are various benefits and allowances that you may be entitled to collect. If you need financial help do not be shy to ask, as it may help give your baby a better start in life. Check with your social worker.

Child Benefit

Fill in the forms for Child Benefit as soon as your baby is born. This benefit is available to every child, and is not affected by how much money parents earn. Sometimes it can be difficult to get the benefits back-dated, so do not delay in completing the form.

Special Benefits

There are other benefits that may be available if your baby has special needs. For example, there is money available to help you if your baby goes home on oxygen.

Your health visitor, GP or paediatrician may also be able to help you by writing to your employer, explaining the situation. This may help to keep your job open for longer, or to increase the time over which maternity benefit is payable.

How Will our Baby Fit into the Immunization Programme?

Getting His Jabs

Your baby will probably have received his first injections before he left the hospital. He will then have a list of dates when you should go to his GP for further injections. Often babies are not given the polio vaccine while they are in hospital, so the full course of vaccinations may be needed.

Ask the hospital staff about immunization before your baby leaves the hospital, and then talk this over with your health visitor and GP.

Ask for a copy of the Action Research Immunization leaflet, which has a timetable that will help to remind you when the next injections are due.

Can I Find Child-care?

Day Care

Most trained child-care specialists should be able to look after your baby, even if he does have special needs. Ask your health visitor if there is anyone in the area who specializes in looking after children who need special care.

Local Support Groups

A Friend in Need

Various local support groups exist specifically to help parents of premature babies. They are normally run by people who have had premature babies and understand just what you are going through at the moment. Ask the neonatal unit staff or your health visitor to write down the local support group phone numbers, and if you like add them to the information page 90 at the back of this book. Don't hesitate to contact them.

Outcome – Look to the Future

Over the past 30 years, more and more premature babies have been surviving. However, premature babies are extremely fragile and even with the greatest care some die and some may be left with a variety of different disabilities.

Survival

Winning the Struggle

Each baby is very different; caring for them in intensive care units is more than simply looking after the physical function of their organs. Part and parcel of each doctor's business is assessing your baby's likely outcome. Do not be afraid to ask doctors and nurses how he is doing — part of their job is to keep you informed of his progress.

As parents you need to appreciate the different risks involved in caring for a child born prematurely. A good doctor will help you to make informed decisions, rather than leave you feeling helpless by making decisions for you.

Catch Up to Term

The Consequences of Being Early

You may start to become confused about how old your baby is. Legally and socially your baby's birthday is the day he was born. However, from a growth and development point of view he should not have been born for another few weeks or months. When doctors are treating your baby they will need to know how old he is relative to the date on which he should have been born.

Over time, the difference between the two dates becomes less important. It will appear as if your baby is catching up with friends of the same age. However, it is not really that he is catching up, but more that any differences are becoming less important.

Let's see why this is:

Born at 28 Weeks:

At his first birthday he will have spent 28 weeks developing inside his mother's womb and a further 52 weeks developing outside; a total of 80 weeks.

Born at Term

At his first birthday he will have spent 40 weeks developing inside and a further 52 weeks developing outside; a total of 92 weeks.

So, at his first birthday a preterm baby has had 15 per cent less time for development compared with a full-term baby.

However, if you repeat this calculation for the two babies when they reach their tenth birthdays, there is very little difference. The term baby has had 560 weeks and the preterm baby has had 548 weeks (2 per cent less) — only a very small difference.

So, Is the Difference Important?

- Over the first year it is very important.
- Over the second year the difference begins to become less significant.

Doctors will usually make corrections to compensate for the fact that a baby has been born prematurely only up until the baby is about two years old.

Does a Premature Birth Delay Childhood Development?

Born at 23 — 24 Weeks:
Development may be delayed and could follow an unusual pattern. However, for many the end result will eventually be the same — a healthy baby.

Born at 29 — 30 Weeks:
There will be very little difference in the pattern of development compared with babies born at term.

Many premature babies may need help from physiotherapists or other specialists at different stages of their childhood. Doctors can help you to find the appropriate assistance when you attend follow-up clinics at the hospital over the next few years.

Disability

The Struggle Continues

The proportion of babies who survive but have a significant disability is again influenced by the age at which they were born.

Age at birth	Chance of baby having a disability
25 weeks	25 per cent
28 weeks	10 per cent
32 weeks	2 per cent

How Many Babies Are Left with Major Disability?

How Many Will Never Be Physically Independent?

At the present time, only four out of every 100 babies born at less than 32 weeks will have a severe disability, and a further six will have minor disabilities.

However, before you get too worried, remember that this means that 90 per cent of all premature babies grow up with no significant disability.

Brain Damage

A Central Concern

Most disability affecting premature babies is due to brain damage. A premature baby's brain is extremely fragile and may become damaged despite even the best care. In fact, in some cases the baby's brain may have been damaged before birth. Sometimes bleeding occurs either into the spaces inside the brain, or into the brain itself, which can result in areas of injury. Doctors will look for signs of this using ultrasound scans.

However, the brain is a remarkable organ. Occasionally large areas will be severely damaged without having any great effect on the behaviour or ability of the baby. What appears to happen is that other areas of the brain can take over the function of the part which has been lost.

Cerebral Palsy

Sometimes the brain cannot compensate for a large proportion of the loss, resulting in some form of disability. In this case the baby is said to have cerebral palsy. This is a general term for disorders of movement and posture resulting from damage to the brain. These disorders are called non-progressive, because they generally do not get worse with age.

The degree of disability is highly variable. Some children are so mildly affected that the condition is only discovered at a clinical examination. Because it is so mild it is unlikely to impair the baby later in life. Other children may be affected severely and may be unable to move at all.

Cerebral palsy is divided into different groups:

- Spastic paralysis:
  abnormal stiffness of the arms and legs, as muscles contract involuntarily
- Athetosis:
  involuntary writhing movements of the limbs
- Ataxia:
  loss of co-ordination and balance.

Learning Difficulties

Some, though by no means all, babies with cerebral palsy also have learning difficulties and may need extra help as they grow up. However, the rest are of average or higher than average intelligence.

Visual Problems

Almost one in 25 very premature babies (born at less than 28 weeks) will develop poor eyesight due to injuries to the back of the eye (the retina). A specialist doctor will check the back of your baby's eyes at regular intervals during his stay on the baby unit.

Although initially it was thought that premature babies became blind or partially sighted because of the high levels of oxygen being given to them, this is now being questioned. We now realize that it is much more complicated and not fully understood yet.

Happy and at home.

Hearing Loss

Two in every 100 premature babies will have some loss of hearing. The cause of this is unknown, but hearing tests may be carried out before your baby goes home or soon after discharge.

Lungs

Babies who are kept on ventilators for a long time may suffer damage to their lungs. This cannot be helped, as without the ventilator your baby's outcome might have been far worse. Doctors have two different names for the problem: Chronic Lung Disease and Bronchopulmonary Dysplasia (BPD).

Over the first few years of life these babies may have many symptoms that are similar to those of asthma. They will have a tendency to wheeze and may be more prone to respiratory infections. Their wheezing will get worse in a dusty or damp atmosphere. Over the years, they usually grow out of the problem as their lungs increase in size. By late childhood, their lungs will usually be completely normal.

Growth and Development

Future Progress

For the first couple of years premature infants may be small, but most will keep to a normal sequence of development. Most premature babies eventually achieve an entirely normal adult height.

However, some may need extra medical help to enable them to grow properly. Monitoring is carried out at hospital Out-patients Clinics throughout their childhood.

By the time premature babies get to their teenage years, most have no problems resulting from the fact that they were born early.

Activity and Posture

Lying There

Recent studies have shown that there may be a link between a baby's posture in the incubator and later physical development. When possible, the baby should lie with normal hip posture and rounded shoulders. It has been suggested that keeping the baby's shoulders forward is associated with improved hand/eye co-ordination later in life.

When your baby goes home he will develop more rapidly if you are able to give him plenty of attention and keep him active. Ask your doctors about things you can do with your baby. There may be particular games that will help to stimulate his development.

Thinking Ahead

Your Baby Has a Future

Most premature babies grow up to be healthy and active members of society. In fact, only one in eight children born prematurely needs some form of extra help when he gets to school. Even then, this help is often only needed to solve some relatively minor problem. If they are given appropriate help, most children will soon overcome these difficulties.

Over the past 20 years great progress has been made in the ability to care for premature babies. The partnership of parents, medical, research and nursing staff using their skills and compassion, and the latest technology ensures that your baby has the best chance for a healthy future. The atmosphere in neonatal units is often intense and stressful, but it is driven by hope — hope for a healthy future for your baby, you, and all of your family.

Glossary of Terms

anaemia having too few red blood cells in the blood. The lack of red blood cells reduces the blood's ability to carry oxygen.

antepartum haemorrhage bleeding from the vagina after 28 weeks of pregnancy. It is most commonly due to some problem with the placenta. It occurs in about 3 per cent of pregnancies.

antibiotics medications used to treat bacterial infections. They work by specifically killing bacteria without harming the person taking them.

apnoea of prematurity (*apnoea* means 'no breathing'). The brains of premature babies may not have developed sufficiently to allow them full control over their breathing. As a result they may stop breathing for a number of minutes. Often they will need some stimulus to help them start again.

arterial lines fine tubes inserted into a baby's artery to monitor his blood pressure and the amount of oxygen in his blood; sometimes these tubes are used to give medication.

asphyxia the condition when the level of oxygen in the blood is too low and the level of carbon dioxide is too high.

bilirubin a yellow pigment released into blood as old red blood cells are broken down. It often gives babies a yellow colour and may need treating by laying the baby under a strong blue light for a few days.

blood gas test a test carried out on a small blood sample to find out how much oxygen and carbon dioxide is in the blood. This gives an indication of how well the lungs, heart and blood vessels are performing.

bronchopulmonary dysplasia (BPD) a complex disorder of the lungs that results from a premature baby needing the help of a ventilator for the first few weeks of life.

brown fat a special type of fat found in babies, located between the shoulder blades and around the kidneys. It is particularly good at generating heat to keep the baby warm.

Cerebrospinal fluid (CSF) Produced in the brain, this fluid normally collects in spaces within the brain (ventricles) and then passes down into the spinal cord where it is eventually absorbed. If the movement of this fluid is blocked it collects inside the head, causing hydrocephalus (*see below*).

colostrum the form of milk produced by a mother within the first few days of her baby's birth. It is thicker and more yellow in colour than the milk that later comes in, and provides vital antibodies and proteins to the baby.

Cytomegalovirus (CMV) a very common type of herpes virus. In most healthy people it produces no symptoms, but it can damage unborn babies.

drip a method of slowly delivering fluids, food or medication directly into a baby's blood vessels.

ECG an electrical recording of a baby's heart. From the tracing doctors can tell a lot about how well the baby is.

electrolytes molecules such as calcium, sodium and potassium that are present in our blood and are essential to life. In caring for a premature baby, it is very important to keep the concentration of electrolytes in his bloodstream under control.

glucose the form of sugar that travels around in our blood and forms a ready supply of energy for the body's cells.

haemoglobin the oxygen-carrying molecule contained in the red blood cells. When haemoglobin is carrying oxygen it is red in colour, when it contains no oxygen it is bluish.

hydrocephalus a build-up of fluid (*hydro*) around the brain (*cephalus*). If it cannot be controlled, it may damage the brain and cause the baby's head to increase in size.

hypertension high (*hyper*) blood pressure (*tension*).

hypoglycaemia a lack (*hypo*) of glucose (*glyc*) in the blood (*aemia*).

intra-ventricular haemorrhage (IVH) bleeding in the brain.

low birth weight (LBW) a birth weight of less than 2,500 g (5½lb).

meconium greenish material that builds up in the baby's bowels before birth. It is usually passed as faeces within 24 hours of birth.

oedema an accumulation of fluid beneath the skin that leads to swelling.

placenta an organ built by the growing baby so that he can get all of the oxygen and nutrients he needs from his mother's blood.

platelets particles that float around in the blood. They are very important in helping blood to clot.

pneumonia Inflammation of the lungs due to an infection.

pre-eclampsia a serious condition in which a pregnant woman suffers from high blood pressure, accumulation of fluid in the tissues and protein in her urine during the second half of pregnancy.

Respiratory distress syndrome (RDS) a lung disorder that affects premature babies. These babies have been born before their lungs are ready to breathe air. They have not started to produce a chemical called surfactant which helps to hold the airways open. It is often treated by giving the baby an artificial surfactant.

saturation monitor a machine that monitors the amount of oxygen there is in a baby's blood.

steroids a group of drugs that mimic some of the body's natural hormones and tend to stimulate cell growth and development.

surfactant a chemical that is present in the lungs of full-term babies and adults which helps to keep the airways open.

ultrasound a machine that uses high-frequency sound waves to detect what is going on in our bodies. These waves can be translated into images that are shown on the screen of the ultrasound machine.

umbilical catheter a small tube inserted into an artery or vein in the baby's umbilical cord. The catheter makes use of the blood vessels which were used by the baby while he was in the womb, but which are no longer required after birth.

urea a waste chemical removed from the body in urine.

ventilator a machine that repeatedly inflates and deflates the baby's lungs. This is used to help babies who are too immature or weak to be able to breathe on their own.

Useful Contact Names and Addresses

Action Research
Vincent House
Horsham
West Sussex
RH12 2DP
Tel: 01403 210406

National Childbirth Trust (NCT)
Alexandra House
Oldham Terrace
Acton
London W3 6NH

Blisslink/Nippers
17–21 Emerald Street
London WC1N 3QL
Tel: 0171–831 0303/8996

Stillbirth and Neonatal Death Society (SANDS)
28 Portland Place
London W1N 4DE

Child Bereavement Trust
1 Millside
Riversdale
Bourne End
Bucks
SL8 5EB

Twins And Multiple Birth Association (TAMBA)
PO Box 30
Little Sutton
South Wirral
L66 1TH

Index

Growth and Development

Dr John Pearce

All parents are interested in their child's emotional, physical and intellectual development.

Growth and Development outlines the stages your child will go through, to reassure and help you to understand your child's unique progress from birth to adolescence.

Taking a look at what influences individual child development, this book covers a wide range of experiences, including:

- The first years of life – developing self–awareness and self–esteem
- The school years – learning how to relate to others, understanding abstract concepts and creative and artistic ability
- Adolescence – learning to cope emotionally and physically with approaching adulthood

In addition to the main sages of development, John Pearce provides information on problem areas such as reading difficulties or bed-wetting which may be causing concern.

ISBN 0 7225 1724 6